JAMES MAY'S Lego House

CONWAY

First published in Great Britain in 2010 by
Conway
An imprint of Anova Books Ltd
10 Southcombe Street
London W14 0RA
www.conwaypublishing.com
www.anovabooks.com

Distributed in the U.S. and Canada by:
Sterling Publishing Co., Inc.
387 Park Avenue South
New York, NY 10016-8810

Produced in association with Plum Pictures Ltd
33 Oval Road, London NW1 7EA

This book was written by James May and Ian Harrison, with contributions from
Christina Fallah and Barnaby Gunning.

A catalogue record for this book is available from the British Library.

10 9 8 7 6 5 4 3 2 1

ISBN 9781844861187

The LEGO® brand name is reproduced with kind permission of The LEGO Group.

The BBC logo is a trade mark of the British Broadcasting Corporation and is
used under licence.
BBC logo © BBC 1996

Edited by Alison Moss
Designed by Steve Russell
Printed and bound by L..E.G.O. s.p.a., Italy

To receive regular email updates on forthcoming Conway titles,
email conway@anovabooks.com with Conway Update in the subject field.

'Lego is a scientific system driven by maths but at the same time it's an endlessly creative system which everyone can understand. There's a numeric logic which means that certain things can happen in Lego and other things definitely can't happen. There's no right or wrong way of doing anything with Lego, but once you master the system you can express anything in it.'

Jørgen Vig Knudstorp, CEO of Lego

'Lego.
You probably have some in your house,
but my house is made of it.'

What I've decided to do is order 3 million Lego bricks and make myself a house. A real house. I'm going to live in it.

It sounds simple. You just clip the bricks together and away you go. But no one has ever done it before – no one has ever built a self-supporting Lego structure that you can actually go inside. So there were lots of questions that would have to be answered before I could build a two-storey Lego house that would not only stand up, but would be one in which I could sit on a Lego chair to eat at my Lego table, walk up my Lego stairs to shower in my Lego shower, and brush my teeth at my Lego basin before going to bed in my Lego bed.

Would I be able to relax and go to sleep? Or would I find myself lying awake all night worrying that the whole thing was going to collapse, and that I'd wake up – or not – buried in Lego?

The architect said he was confident it would work, telling me: 'You should wake up at the same height you go to sleep.'

I couldn't help noticing that he used the word 'should', not 'will'...

Location, Location, Location

Among the first questions to be answered were: where should I build my house, and what style should I build it in?

My first idea was to build it in a vacant plot on an ordinary urban street, but it soon became apparent that I was going to have all sorts of problems with security and with planning permission: no local authority would give me permission, even when I promised them it would be brick built.

Then it occurred to me that I've never lived in the country, because I don't really understand the countryside, so I decided to give it a try: my Lego house could be my country retreat. Denbies Wine Estate in Surrey was quite happy to have me, and I'm quite interested in drinking wine, so it seemed like the perfect solution from my point of view. But maybe not from Denbies' point of view. They'll be finding Lego bricks among the vines for years to come, and I can't help wondering whether that will affect the *terroir* – it might give the wine a rather angular quality.

A True Lego House

Anyway, I invited Barnaby Gunning, my chosen architect, to come and view the site. He was slightly concerned about the sloping ground but that's an inevitable part of building in a vineyard – vines like a slope. So we decided that the house should look as if it had grown out of the slope – as if it had emerged out of the earth and the slope had fallen away below it.

'As if we've peeled back the grass to reveal the Lego beneath?' asked Barnaby.

'Yes,' I agreed, warming to the theme. 'As if the world is a great big ball of Lego and the house is a bit that's just poked through the surface.'

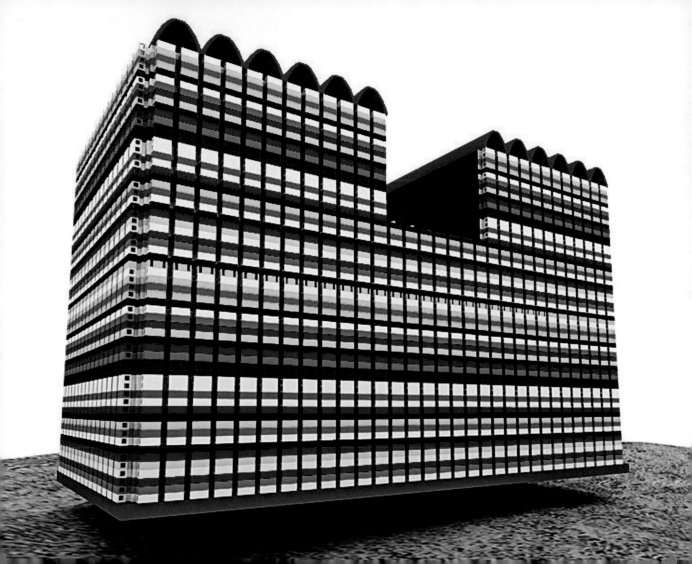

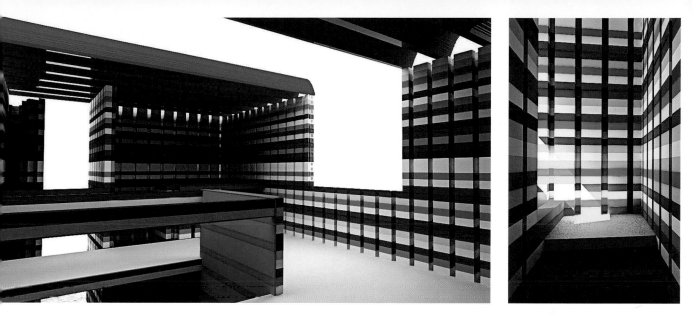

But that didn't help us decide what it should look like. I didn't want to make a Lego house like a scaled up kit; I didn't want it to be a Lego representation of some tiresome Georgian pile. I wanted something very modern; something specifically designed to be made from Lego rather than something designed as a house that we then happen to make from Lego. If we were to design a house that played to the strengths of Lego and avoided its weaknesses we would get a specific type of house, an inherently Lego house, in the way that the design of concrete houses, brick houses and wooden houses all reflect the properties of the materials they are made from.

**In other words, I didn't want a house made of Lego,
I wanted a Lego house, which is subtly different.**

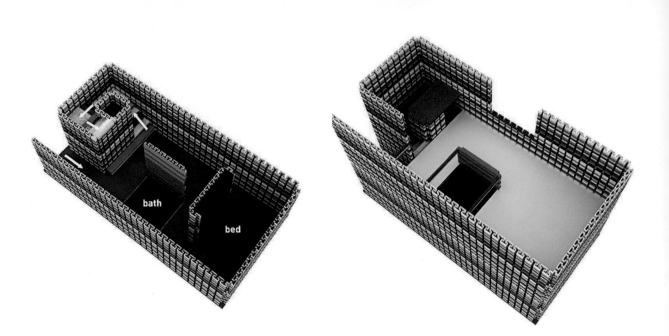

Barnaby's Initial Design

James and I spent a day looking at other houses. My first observation had been that although Lego is best known as a 'construction toy', its greatest merit lies in its ability to come apart easily, and so our design would need to take advantage of Lego's ability to lock together, and avoid elements that would tear themselves apart if built in Lego. Forces that push things together are referred to as compression; pulling apart is known as tension. My suspicion was that we would need to think about structures that worked purely on compression. Towards the end of the day we visited a ruined abbey. Stone, like Lego, when used completely in compression, is an excellent building material. Stone structures can last for thousands of years. Perhaps the house would need to be built with a domed roof, buttresses, vaults and arches?

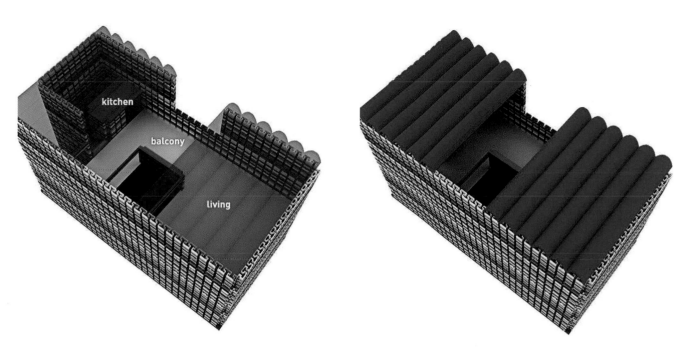

My first design had the smaller rooms (bedroom, bathroom and entrance) on the ground floor so that they could support a larger living room on the first floor, most of which would be covered by a roof of arched strips. (See also previous pages.) The first suggestion for building the walls was to create a kind of 'Greek key' pattern with a single skin of Lego bricks. The overall thickness of the wall would appear to be nearly 20 centimetres, although its actual thickness would be only 16 millimetres. Light would filter into the building through tall strips of see-through bricks. The dimension of the undulating pattern was set to coincide with the prototype Lego beam size being worked on by Neil Thomas and Eva Wates of Atelier One, so that the walls and beams would lock together precisely. However, initial tests showed that this structure would not be strong enough.

The Lego Vernacular

Barnaby christened our revolutionary and as-yet-unresolved architectural style the Lego vernacular. He imagined a body of architecture growing to include modular Lego houses that could be stacked together to make Lego apartment blocks. That reminded me of a friend of mine who, as a child, had a Lego kit of a house. Sometimes she would use the bricks as intended, to build the house, but sometimes she would treat each brick like a separate house and spread them out to make a city of miniature houses. Both hers and Barnaby's ideas played on the incontrovertible logic of Lego, Barnaby expanding the logic outwards, imagining a complete house as a component of something larger, and my friend contracting it inwards, using the components of her house as complete units in themselves.

These two concepts gave me an idea for the design of the house: it should be based on the proportions of the eighter brick (the one with 8 studs), which was the foundation stone of the entire Lego universe. It was an elegant idea, and if it turned out that the answer to the Lego house lay in the Lego brick itself that would be highly satisfying.

Pick 'n' Mix

But before I could start building my house, I was going to need some bricks to build it with. Working out how many elements of each type and colour to order was tricky given that the house still only existed as a rough sketch, so I had simply made an educated guess at the minimum I would require and ordered that. As the design was refined I would order more. You can't buy more than about 3 million in one go anyway because nobody stocks that amount; not even the factory. In fact, when I tried to order another 500,000 from the factory a few weeks later they didn't have enough, so in the end the house was made up of 3.3 million elements.

The next question was: how long would it take to put 3 million elements together?

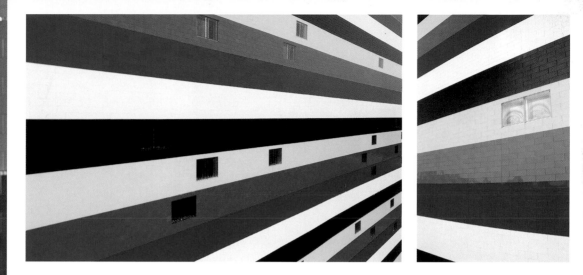

Builder's Estimate

Professional contractors can make estimates based on their existing knowledge of how long it takes a brickie to build a wall, or a cement mixer to pour cement. But no one had ever built Lego on this scale before, so there was no official measure or quantification of how long it takes to build life-size walls out of Lego – and I needed to know that in order to work out how long it would take to build a house. So I got three pairs of volunteers and gave them all two hours to build a wall with a window in it.

The end result was three very interesting-looking walls of varying degrees of flimsiness. But the frightening thing was just how much slower it was than I'd imagined; so slow, in fact, that I was starting to worry about whether we'd ever be able to build a house. All three teams had managed to build a passable wall but none of them was more than 3 feet square — and that was nothing compared to the size of a house.

We were going to need either hundreds and hundreds of days or hundreds and hundreds of people – or both. Even if 1,000 people put together 1,000 bricks each we would still only be a third of the way there. It was clear that the only way we were going to get the house built would be to design a modular building block and to get a very large team of people making these blocks on a production line off site. The blocks could then be ferried up to the site and the actual house should go together relatively quickly using those prefabricated components.

So Barnaby designed a standard modular component and I put out an appeal to the great British public.

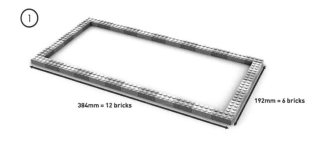

384mm = 12 bricks

192mm = 6 bricks

use stretcher bond

34 bricks per course

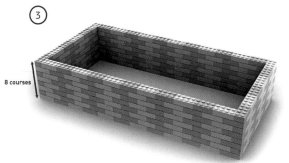

8 courses

272 bricks per component

The Modular Block

The response was phenomenal. There were so many enquiries that we had to put out a second appeal for people to stay away because we weren't going to have room for them all. Despite that more than 4,000 people turned up at Denbies from as far afield as Birmingham, and queued from 5.30 in the morning to help build the Lego breeze blocks from which the house would be constructed. Unfortunately we only had room for 1,100 volunteers but they worked like Trojans and built about 4,000 breeze blocks in various colours.

At last, construction of the Lego house had begun and it seemed as if it could actually become a reality.

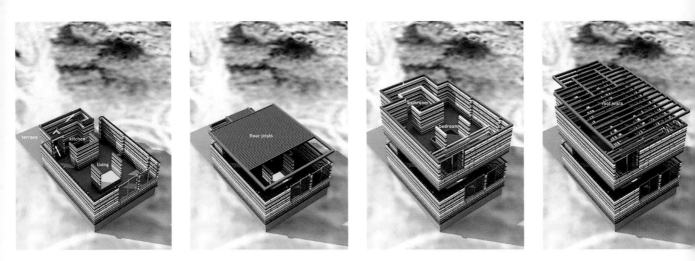

Two by Two by Two

In the meantime the design had evolved considerably. It was still based on the idea of the house being a giant version of a standard eighter, and Barnaby explained how he had developed the concept: 'One of the things I immediately noticed about the Lego brick is it has this strange mathematical logic where the dimensions of the brick scale up in multiples of two.'

This I already knew: Duplo bricks are double the length, height and width of a standard Lego brick, hence the name Duplo. But they are actually eight times as big as a standard brick because 2 x 2 x 2 = 8.

pyramid roof elements

'On the same principle,' Barnaby continued, 'if you multiply each of the dimensions by 256, which is two times itself eight times, you get a shape which is about two metres in height from floor to floor. That's not a bad size for a house: slightly smaller than usual but quite nice. The fact that it's scaled up from a standard brick means that I can show you a very simple 1:256 scale model of the exterior of the house.'

And with that he clipped two eighters on top of each other and handed them to me: 'Here's your model.'

It was genius.

Octuplo

Not only was I going to be living in a Lego house, I was going to be living in two stacked eighters scaled up by two to the power of eight. You can keep your seventh heaven: here was paradise in eights. I would call it Octuplo, even though each storey of the house would actually be 256 x 256 x 256 = 16.8 million times the size of a standard brick. It meant, as I had expected all along, that the shape of the building was going to be very plain and austere – very brick-like, in fact – but that plainness was more than made up for by the design details and the colour scheme.

Primary Colours

My first instinct had been that the colours should be quite random, because the random and chaotic nature of the mixing of Lego bricks is part of what Lego is about. But having seen Barnaby's visualisations I decided that I liked the idea of his more formal scheme – stripes of colour in the courses of the blockwork, or panels of colour à la Piet Mondrian. In the end, we settled on a mixture: stripes of colour for the exterior walls, bold blocks of red for two of the interior supporting walls and a random assortment for the third. But the randomness of that third interior wall had to be enlarged to suit the size of the house; if individual Lego bricks had been arranged randomly it would have made no visual sense at all. So each modular block was a single colour but those blocks were arranged randomly, thus scaling up the randomness so that the rhythm of randomness was as it should be.

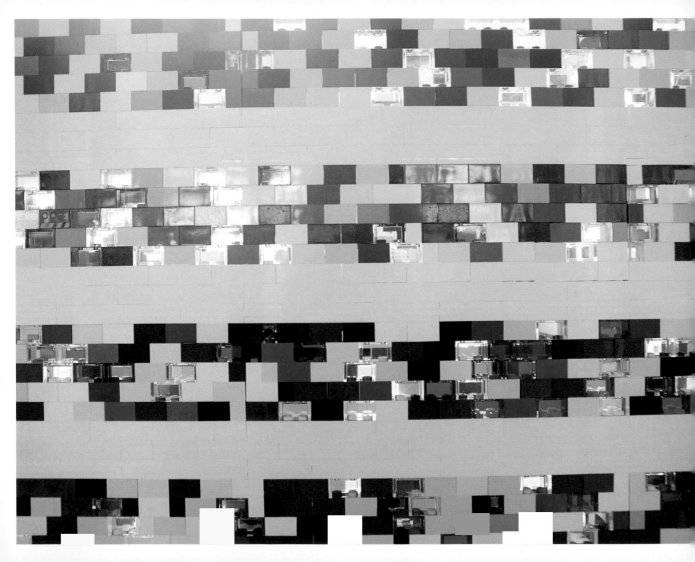

DIVAN
GROUND FLOOR
WD-1919mm
HT-400mm
DP-1150mm

'We should think of a new Lego design language.
...I've said "design language" now!'

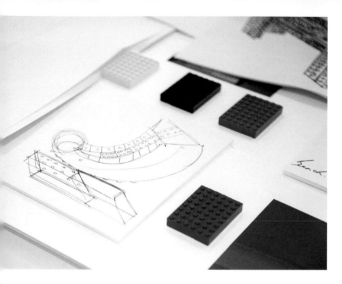

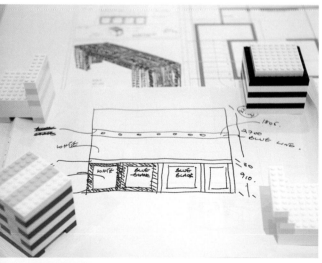

Christina's Interior Design

One of the first things I did when I joined the project as interior designer was to request for actual Lego pieces to be sent to my office so that I could 'play' with it myself. Being brought up on Barbie dolls and not having any previous experience with Lego, my approach, as far as the Lego experts were concerned, was pretty amateurish.

I made and played with pieces of Lego, experimenting as to how to make a table, chair, chess pieces, and the like. In reality I was flying by the seat of my pants! But it was the only way to learn – by trial and error. My ultimate objective was to make sure that the pieces of furniture looked and functioned like furniture, and were not pastiches of Legoland and Lego Denmark.

From a conceptual point of view my ideas and inspiration were immediately Mondrian, Postmodernism and Cubism. Barnaby and I were in agreement right from the beginning as to the glasslikeness of working with Lego and the concealment of the studs, as well as the wide horizontal bands of colour.

We incorporated this concept into the furniture as well as the walls, and used strong patterns so that the pieces would stand out. Hence striped kitchen chairs accompany the black table with a bright yellow herringbone design. Had these taken a more random pattern and similar colours to the perimeter walls, they would have been lost.

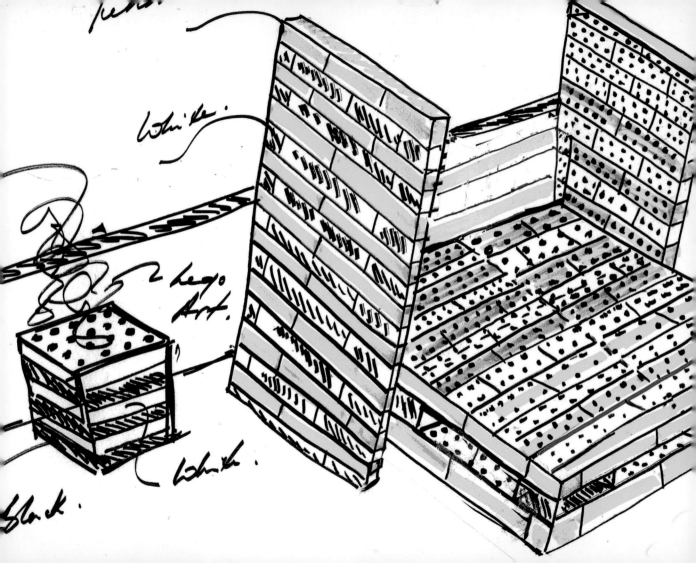

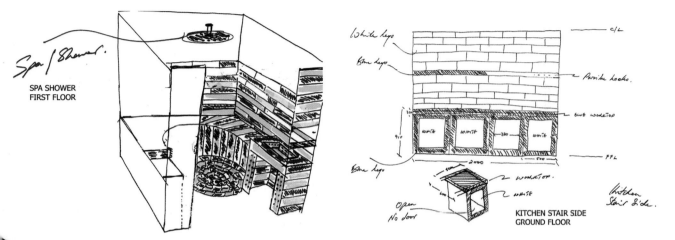

Spa / Shower.

SPA SHOWER
FIRST FLOOR

White legs

Blue legs

Provide hooks.

c/L

Blue worktop

WHITE | WHITE | 380 | WHITE

900

300

FFL

Blue legs

2000 | 500

Open
No door

Worktop.
White.

Kitchen
Stair Side.

KITCHEN STAIR SIDE
GROUND FLOOR

My sketches are all quite colourful and childlike: I remember using lots of coloured markers at the outset, rather than a restrictive Autocad-based computer drawing package. I was adamant that I needed to draw by hand as I was working with my hands when making the models. It seemed the most natural method at the time and I believe strongly that the images have taken on a childlike quality, rather than being precise and technical.

24-26 PEOPLE

UPRIGHT

BLUE +

YELLO

4 STUD OVERHANG
ON SEAT!

WHITE (×6) 8 STUDS.

18 BRICKS
HIGH.

54 STUDS.

Form follows Function

This is one of the actual kitchen chairs in blue and white. The large-scale stripes leant boldness and played on the general colour scheme. The sketch was drawn by Lego enthusiast Kevin Cooper. What no one thought about in the initial sketch and model was the structural implication of the chair so when it came to testing it, James was repeatedly making it collapse! In the end I had to remake the seat, back and base in a completely different way using flat plates and a waffle system that was concealed inside the blocks of colour.

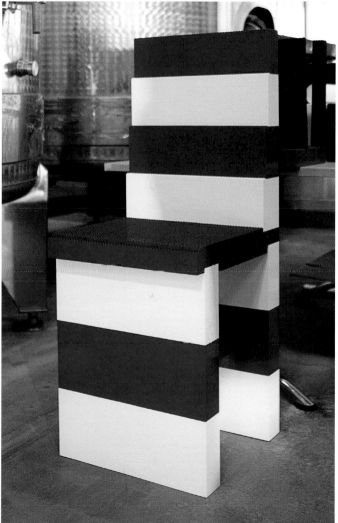

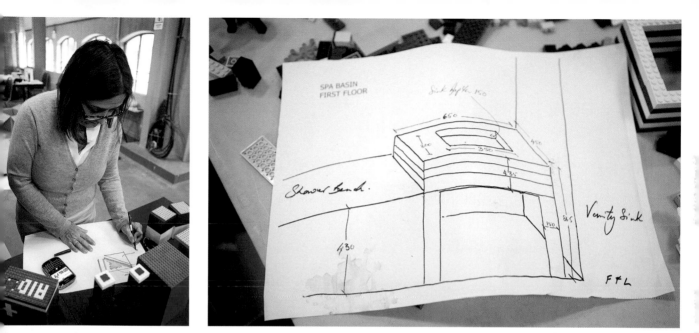

SPA BASIN
FIRST FLOOR

Sink Hgt to 150

650

200

350

450

Shower Bench.

435

150

865

430

Vanity Sink

FFL

One of the most complicated features was the Union flag, from hand-drawing a sketch using reference on the internet, to setting it out to work on back to back with bricks and then transporting the whole thing up to the house to become the dividing wall between the bedroom and the bathroom. Other challenging pieces were the toilet and the red swivel chair. Kevin Cooper was the brains behind these. He painstakingly built both without cheating so that they could be used properly. I was particularly impressed with Kevin's ingenious ideas for the cistern and water tank and for making the toilet waterproof by lining it with Vaseline.

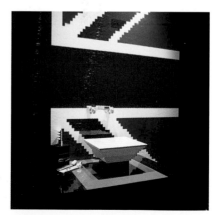

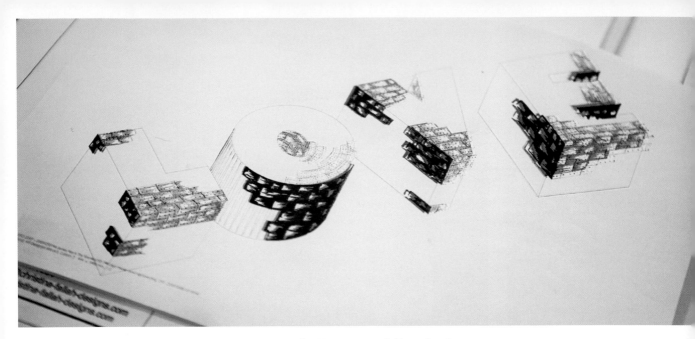

Letters and Symbols

When using multi-coloured Lego bricks it can prove a challenge to the viewer to identify the specific object against a monochromatic background. Because of this difficulty I designed the kitchen appliances and utensils for the viewer to be able to recognise an object or brand instantly. Words were blocked, for example, 'chop' across the chopping board; 'jug' on a pouring implement; 'ice' on the fridge. Sometimes a simple letter was used, such as 'S' and 'P' for salt and pepper.

For branded commodities a different approach was taken. Blocked colours and shape were used for classic designs of sauce bottles and soup cans, and yellow numbers against a black background made the association with the Heinz 57 varieties.

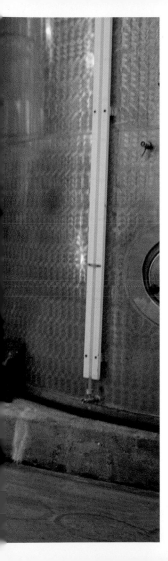

Counting Bricks

Once I had gathered enough information to sketch out a floor plan working with the perimeter outlines provided by Barnaby, we set out creating the furniture layouts, lighting layouts and information for presentation to James and then to the crew on site for the build.

When the CAD plans (see overleaf) had been signed off, I was in a position to list how many pieces of furniture were required for the actual build, so that we could establish how much labour was needed, how long we would be on site, and how many bricks we would need. We counted bricks over and over again.

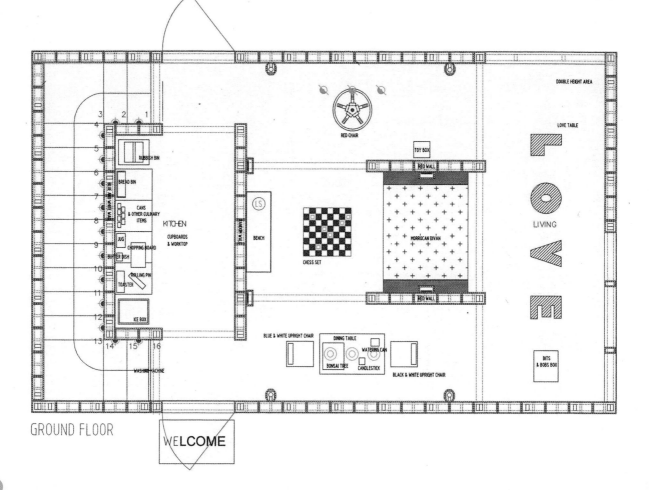

RED CHAIR

DOUBLE HEIGHT AREA

LOVE TABLE

3 2 1
4
RUBBISH BIN

5

BREAD BIN

6

7
CANS
& OTHER CULINARY
ITEMS

KITCHEN

8

JUG

9
CHOPPING BOARD

BUTTER DISH

10
ROLLING PIN

TOASTER

11

12
ICE BOX

13

14 15 16

WASHING MACHINE

CUPBOARDS
& WORKTOP

BLUE AND WHITE WALL

DIVIDING WALL

LS

BENCH

CHESS SET

TOY BOX

RED WALL

MORROCAN DIVAN

RED WALL

LIVING

BITS
& BOBS BOX

BLUE & WHITE UPRIGHT CHAIR

DINING TABLE

WATERING CAN

BONSAI TREE

CANDLESTICK

BLACK & WHITE UPRIGHT CHAIR

GROUND FLOOR

WELCOME

56

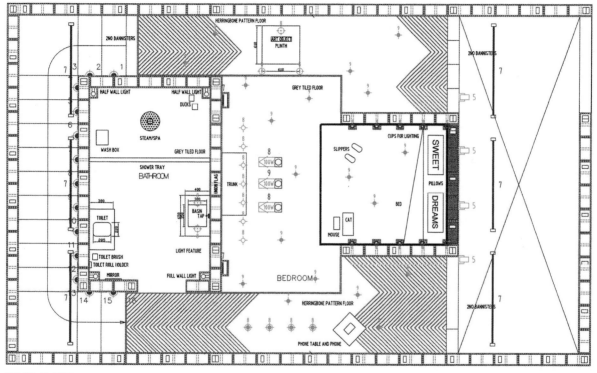

HERRINGBONE PATTERN FLOOR

2NO BANNISTERS

ART OBJECT
PLINT

610

610

7 3

2 1

HALF WALL LIGHT   HALF WALL LIGHT

DUCKS

STEAM/SPA

WASH BOX   GREY TILED FLOOR

GREY TILED FLOOR

2NO BANNISTERS

7

5

CUPS FOR LIGHTING

SWEET

SLIPPERS

PILLOWS

1

6

SHOWER TRAY
BATHROOM

7

TRUNK

8
100W

9
100W

8
100W

5

DREAMS

7

BED

CAT

HOUSE

5

300

200

BASIN
TAP

TOILET

285

285

11

LIGHT FEATURE

BEDROOM

5

7

TOILET BRUSH
TOILET ROLL HOLDER

2

MIRROR

7 3   FULL WALL LIGHT

14   15   16

HERRINGBONE PATTERN FLOOR

PHONE TABLE AND PHONE

2NO BANNISTERS

7

FIRST FLOOR

'This truly is how all houses should be built. The walls are quite literally leaping up at an astonishing rate.'

Bricking it

So: we had a design, we had several thousand modular blocks, and we had a team of people in the winery making furniture, fittings and specialist parts. The components would be ferried up the hill and assembled on site – it would be just like making a Lego kit, except that the bricks would be bigger. And in theory it would be much quicker than building with bricks and mortar because we wouldn't have to mix cement, slap it on, and align each course of bricks using string and a spirit level. Lego is automatically level, and the integrity of Lego is such that once you've established the footprint you know it will go together: it has to, it's an immutable law of Lego. There's no way you can get half way up and then find that the Lego doesn't fit any more because any Lego brick fits with any other Lego brick. Which was quite reassuring because it meant that nothing could go wrong.

Except that something did go wrong.

When it came to signing off the engineer's drawings we discovered that no one would insure the building because there was no existing data on Lego as a building material, which meant that no one could confirm that it was safe. We had thoroughly tested our components with bags of gravel that cumulatively weighed far more than I do, so we knew that our structure would work, but that was not enough. With a conventional building you can do structural calculations using an accumulation of knowledge about your materials, but no one had ever used Lego as a building material so that accumulated knowledge was not available. Which meant there was no way of doing the calculations. The drawings couldn't be signed off without insurance, and the insurers insisted on the building having a wooden frame, because there is an accumulation of knowledge about the strength of wood. But that completely defeated our object of using Lego as a building material.

I was devastated. It looked as if we would have to start the entire design again from scratch. But then Barnaby came up with an ingenious solution: stick to our basic design but build it around the wooden frame without touching it, so that the frame would be there as a safety net if any of the Lego structure failed, but the Lego structure itself would still be largely self-supporting.

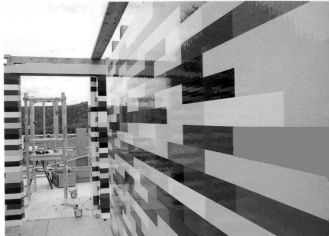

So that's what we did. The frame was erected and the Lego blocks were slotted over the wooden uprights, which stood like a skeleton within the cavities of the Lego brickwork. The only real structural concession was that the upper floor was supported by wooden joists instead of Lego ones but otherwise the house remained true to itself – and at least we knew that Lego joists would have done the same job even if the insurers refused to take our word for it.

So it was still a Lego house, and when I was inside it I would still be walking on Lego, sitting on Lego, leaning on Lego and lying on Lego. And relieving myself on Lego, if my Lego toilet was progressing according to plan. It would certainly put a new spin on the phrase 'bricking it'...

The Lego House holds the Guinness World Record for the largest Lego structure.

'What I'm actually doing here is answering a question I asked myself as a 6-year-old boy. If you had enough Lego bricks, could you build yourself a Lego house?

Yes you could.
Here it is.'

Moving in (for one night only)

They say that moving into a new house is one of the most stressful days of a person's life, but as I walked through the rows of Chardonnay on a glorious September morning I was really looking forward to it.

The house looked absolutely stupendous with its bold stripes and multi-faceted roof catching the morning light; with its vibrant primary plastic colours perfectly offsetting the natural green of the vines. And the view from the outside was nothing compared to the cornucopia of Lego treats that lay inside.

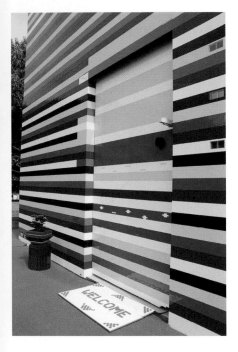

True to homeowning tradition, the Lego key was hidden under the Lego flowerpot next to the Lego doormat. I inserted the key in the lock, slid it to the side, opened the Lego door (hung on Lego Technics hinges) and stepped over the threshold. It was like entering another dimension.

This was my childhood fantasy come true. I was overwhelmed by Lego. This wasn't like stepping into a massive house made out of Lego, it was like being shrunk and stepping into a tiny Lego-scale house. Everything was Lego. Walls, floor, chairs, tables, newspaper. Cat. Light fittings. A kitchen with Lego toaster, Lego washing machine, Lego cutlery and utensils, even a Lego salad and an open bar of Lego chocolate.

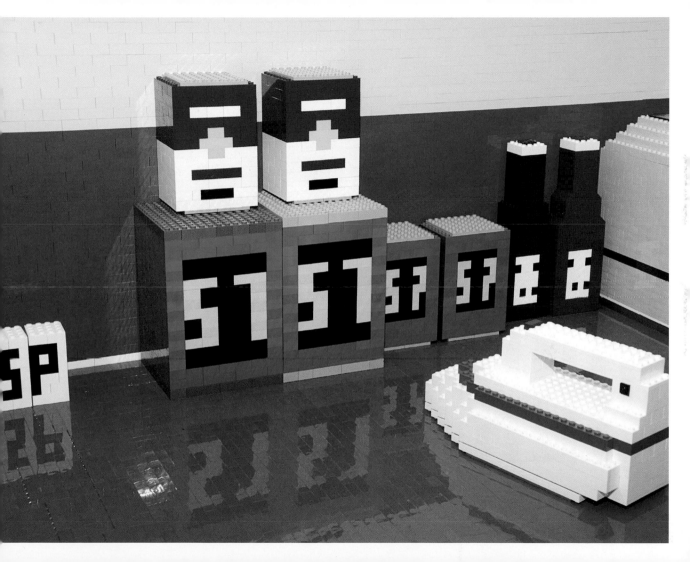

Upstairs the imagination and wit of the people who had made these things continued to overflow everywhere I looked. The volunteers who had come up with all the ideas for Lego clutter and the Lego trappings of everyday Lego life, had excelled themselves. The fact that upstairs existed at all was amazing enough – I had originally thought we might manage a bungalow or a beach hut – but the details took it to another level. The Lego bed was made with Lego sheets and Lego pillows, and there was even a pair of Lego slippers. Next to the Lego basin in the Lego bathroom was a Lego razor, Lego toothbrush and flattened Lego tube of toothpaste; there was a working Lego shower and next to that the *pièce de resistance* – a stunningly engineered Lego toilet, complete with flushing mechanism and ball-cock all painstakingly made from Lego.

In short, it was a triumph. Barnaby's achievement in creating the structure was matched only by that of interior designer Christina Fallah and her team of volunteers in creating the furniture, fittings and lighting. When I looked in the Lego mirror I expected to see the face of a 6-year-old boy looking back at me. I was living a childhood dream.

There's a very postmodern feel to this.
I'm not always aware that I'm looking
at Lego until I get close to it.

Paul Nelson, Surrey University for the Creative Arts

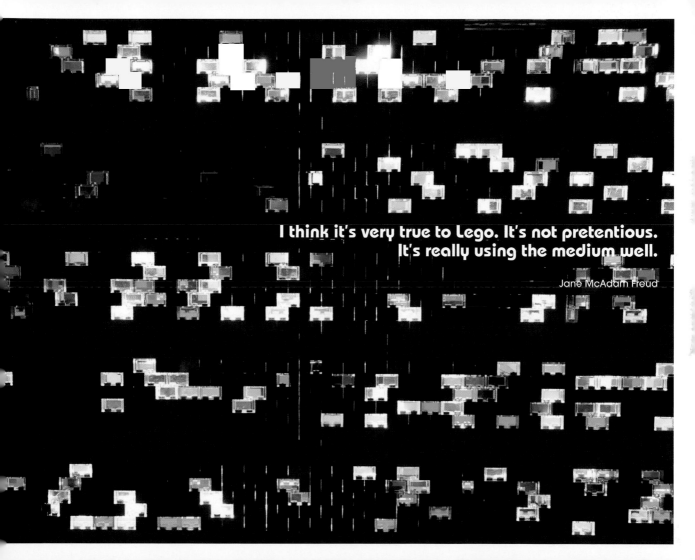

I think it's very true to Lego. It's not pretentious.
It's really using the medium well.

Jane McAdam Freud

Housewarming

The reality of being in the house was better than I had ever imagined it could be, by a factor of ten. And it was about to get even better, as the guests started arriving for my housewarming party. Gerald Scarfe arrived with a caricature of me – done in Lego of course – to hang on the wall; Jane Asher arrived in time to convince me that I was not going to be able to prepare food for 20 guests in a kitchen with no cooker, and then Oz Clarke arrived bearing the all-important wine, which I insisted we decant into a Lego bottle.

My other guests included other participants in the *Toy Stories* television series: Jane McAdam Freud, who had helped me unleash my creativity on the Plasticine garden; Tiff Needell, my roving reporter on the historic Scalextric race; and several of the Liverpool University students who had helped build the Meccano bridge.

And so to Bed...

Now came the real measure of my new house – how soundly would I sleep? The bed was hard, but not unpleasant (an opinion I would revise by morning) but the Lego sheets proved to be purely ornamental. So I curled up under my luxurious red blanket and turned off the lights.

I was about to become the first person in history to spend the night in a Lego house. Despite Barnaby's reticence all those months earlier I was confident that I would wake up at the same height I went to sleep. I expected that my dreams would be angular and primary coloured. As I drifted towards sleep I couldn't shake off the sensation that I had passed through some hole in the space time continuum and that I might now be forever in the land of Lego; that when I woke up the following morning the sun would be made of Lego, and the clouds.

And so I fell asleep with the thought that if it was ever overcast in my Lego world I would be able to dismantle the clouds and remake them as a battleship, or a cat, or a piano, or a green Citroën 2CV like the one my mother used to drive...

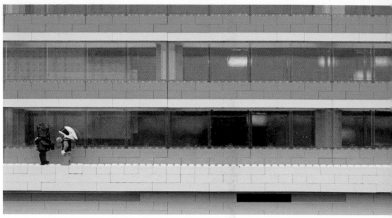

Acknowledgements

With grateful thanks to Christina Fallah (www.christina-fallah-designs.com), Barnaby Gunning (www.barnabygunning.com), The LEGO Group (www.lego.com), Plum Pictures, Denbies Wine Estate, Atelier One, Lightplan, Kevin Cooper and all the volunteers who helped to build the house. And to Barnaby's children, who took their Lego people to visit the Lego House!

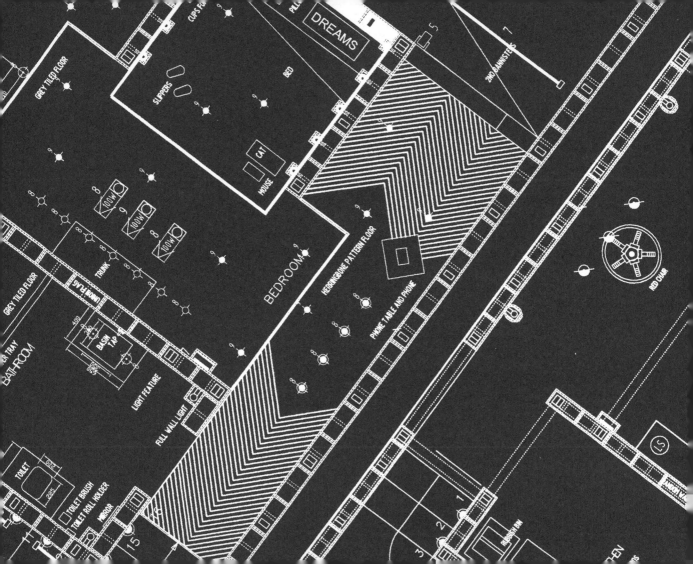